Your Sensual Awakening

Awakening

A Month Long Journey of Self-Discovery

S. R. Lee

ISBN: 1719098255
ISBN-13: 9781719098250

DEDICATION

To all the woman all over the world who take up space and shine with an inner light. To those of you whose beauty is an irresistible blend of confidence, kindness, and lust for life, something so much deeper than the skin….you who made me think to myself,
"I want what SHE has." …..
I humbly and gratefully dedicate this to you.

CONTENTS

FOREWARD

Welcome to "Your Sensual Awakening", and congratulations on taking this step to honor and appreciate the woman that you are! I am so excited to have you on this month long journey and hope that your sensual quest continues to evolve with the completion of the course.

Remember, re-establishing open communication with your inner sex kitten can at times seem a daunting task. I strongly encourage the actual participation and completion of each of the daily "soul work" assignments, as I like to call them, as it is *action* rather than simply reading over them, which will facilitate the greatest results. That being said, be gentle with yourself. You have already taken such a large step in your quest for personal pleasure and empowerment. As you navigate this next months adventures, I would like you to remember that you are your own best friend, (even if you are not used to relating to yourself in this way, you can start right now!). Please do not say or think anything harsh or critical about yourself that you would not say to a dear friend or loved one. And if you find that you have skipped a day or are feeling stuck and frustrated about not making the progress you had hoped for, do not despair! You ARE making a change! You ARE at this very moment, in the process of transformation. Just as the caterpillar undergoes unseen changes while hidden within her chrysalis before emerging as a butterfly, or the way the water begins flowing beneath the frozen surface of a winter stream before the cracks appear on the ice, completely hidden from outside observation, so too is your evolution a delicate process which takes time. How much time is largely dependent on the individual and their commitment to their blossoming, but there is no right or wrong way to go about it. Any change, no matter how small, is progress, and each woman is different in her development. What remains the same is that it cannot be rushed. One would not think of breaking the butterfly out of her chrysalis before she is ready, or attempting to melt the surface of a frozen stream with a blow dryer before the springtime thaw! The first lesson to internalize about your inner Sensual Goddess is that she is never rushed! She takes her time, delights in the process, soaks in and relishes each and every moment, savoring it like a sip of fine wine, and arrives exactly when she means to. She adheres to no ones schedule except maybe that of the moon. Her own inner clock is attuned to the rhythm of her heart, and moves in cyclical rather than linear paths. Your eventual embodiment of your Sensual Goddess is a natural and gradual process. Focus on the journey, on your small daily victories, and before you know it, you will be dancing through the world with a seductive sparkle in your eye and earthy sway in your hips. You will have welcomed Sensual Goddess home. You will have truly integrated your Sensual Awakening.

Keep in mind that while becoming reacquainted with your inner sensual goddess may seem close to impossible at first, it does get easier with time. That is because being a vibrant, sexy, sensual, pleasure loving, life celebrating being is *natural!* You are already a sensual goddess. There is no crazy skill to learn or persona to develop. Rather, it is largely about uncovering the intimate relationship you already have with your own sexuality, one which has likely been swamped and neglected by our fast paced, linear, logical, and predominantly masculine, western culture. While there are multiple benefits that come from living in our modern society, we have unfortunately forgotten how to nurture and respect our sacred femininity, and countless men and woman have suffered for it. By re-acquainting your self with your Sensual Goddess, you are healing not only yourself, but a wounded culture of sexual misunderstanding and perversion. Thank you for your sacred work!

I refer to the Sensual Goddess in the third person to make it easier to relate to this aspect of ourselves that we may be largely unfamiliar with. But she is already here within you. She is a part of you and you are part of her. That is why you are participating in this course now. It is both your doing and her doing. You and your Sensual Goddess are one and the same, and you have already taken the first large step in re-establishing your relationship together. You are both deeply invested in this awakening.

To further honor the commitment you have made to yourself and your inner Goddess, I recommend keeping a special 'Sensual Awakening Diary'. You will use this diary to record your thoughts and feelings as you progress through the course. It is a wonderful way to give expression to your energy as it changes and arises, and also a great tool for tracking your growth and progress as a brilliant, sensual being.

And so, without further adieu, we begin:

WEEK 1: GETTING PRESENT IN THE NOW

The first skill we must learn if we want to awaken our inner Sensual Goddess is to get present in the Now. This may seem to be a comically simple task, but take a moment to think about it and you will realize that a large portion of our days, (dare I say a majority), are taken up thinking about the past or the future. More often than not, this thought process is one of worry, stress, or regret. We bemoan past experiences, replaying them over and over again subconsciously in our minds, and worry about the future; the security of our jobs, the health of our children, the upcoming bills, the laundry list of chores needing to get done, what to cook for dinner, will we have time to make love to our partners? Do we even want to? All of these things, even if they *are* positive in nature, take us away from the Now and out of the present moment.

While it is necessary to think about the future from time to time, in order to function as a responsible adult in todays society, and revisiting the past can sometimes be beneficial, as we are able to learn from past experiences and even find pleasure in remembering a past event, dwelling in either is unhealthy and damaging to the relationship with your Sensual Goddess. The current moment is all that really exists. The past and the future are mere thought projections into non-existent scenarios. We are never in past, we are never in the future, we are only in the Now, in this current moment. So to spend so much energy focused on what is *not* rather than what *is,* is counter productive and borderline madness. Don't blame yourself. Our preoccupation with escaping the now is something that has been instilled in us since birth, just as it was in our parents and their parent before them. This cultural mental ailment is something that has been going on for generations. There is no point crying about it or pointing fingers, (remember, the past is in the past!), but we can learn from it and choose to grow from it starting right this instant.

Sensual Goddess does not dwell in the past or worry about the future. She is deeply rooted in the Now. She savors and enjoys each current moment in all its sensual glory. She is fully open to all of lifes' beautiful experiences, and finds beauty and grace even in the moments that are not so wonderful. Whatever her current situation or experience, she embraces it fully and courageously, and finds the silver lining in any circumstance simply by allowing its full integration into her being. Sound confusing? Not so! Picture yourself stuck in traffic on the I405 during rush hour. You've been working all day. You need to get home to make dinner, for yourself and maybe your family. You have a long list of chores to do before tomorrow and no idea how they are going to get done in time. And now traffic is at a stand still. To make matters worse some a-hole just zoomed up the shoulder and rudely cut you off, so close he almost clipped your bumper! You feel your shoulders tense, your jaw clenches, your fists grip the steering wheel, and your heart rate accelerates. You feel a hot and bubbling anger and agitation stirring in your belly. As your car inches along the hot freeway, your level of stress continues to rise until it is almost overwhelming. By the time you arrive home, hours after you expected, you are on the verge of tears. In times such as these it is helpful to think; WWSGD- What Would Sensual Goddess do?

By imagining the above scenario we can see that much of the irritation comes from projecting ourselves out of the current moment and into the future one, the one where we must cook dinner, finish a work assignment, get the kids ready for bed and clean the house all before morning. We are spending too much time dwelling in a mental state of being which is far removed from our actual reality of being stuck in traffic. While it may be necessary to think about the things that need to get done, Sensual Goddess stops worrying about them the instant she realizes they are beyond her control. She may call up her spouse and ask him or her to order take out, she may call her children on her blue tooth to ask them about their day and let them know she is going to be home later than expected, she may even mourn the fact that the laundry is going to sit in a pile on the bedroom floor for yet another night. And *then*- she

RELAXES! Thats right, right there on the good ol' 405 Freeway, she leans back and smiles. She turns on her favorite music or maybe a podcast she has been wanting to listen to but hasn't found the time for. Perhaps she sprays a mist of sweet smelling perfume or air freshener. She takes full, deep breaths and notes the way the sunlight feels as it falls on her arms and legs, kissing her with its warmth. She looks up and admires the shapes of the clouds as they drift across a brilliantly blue sky. What are those pretty bushes that have been planted on the side of the freeway? And how sexy are the curves of the mountain ridge visible in the distance? As she inches her way home, she might use the opportunity to sing at the top of her lungs, something she is not yet comfortable doing around others. Or maybe she gives herself a loving self-massage, rubbing out the tension in her neck, shoulders, arms, and legs. She may find joy in observing the stoic faces of the drivers around her, delighting in the diversity of the human face and expression. When another driver catches her staring, she offers up a genuine smile. Perhaps it is returned, and maybe it is not. Either way, Sensual Goddess realizes she has a choice; She can allow herself to become agitated by a situation that is beyond her control, and continue to focus on all the things she feels she needs to do in the future, despite being powerless to do anything about it in the current situation, or she can choose to make the current moment as enjoyable for herself as possible, even if it's not quite drinking fruit cocktails at the day-spa. Sensual Goddess always chooses pleasure and enjoyment over stress and worry, whenever possible. And in order to do this, it is necessary to become fully aware of the Now.

Day 1-Meditation

Ahh yes. I can hear the groans from here. I know for many meditation has been more of a headache than a tool for sensuality, but it is no coincidence that the Dali Lama has stated "If every 8 year old in the world was taught how to mediate, all the worlds problems would be wiped out in one generation".

I firmly believe meditation (along with Tantra, which is essentially the merging of meditation and sex!), is HUGELY underrated and also the key to self acceptance, love, peace, and inner joy. It is also the foundation of basically every religion and belief system in existence, be it called meditation, prayer, trance, or magic.

So what exactly *is* meditation? Put simply meditation is the quieting of the mind and immersion in the moment. It is not about sitting in the lotus position under a tree for hours on end without moving a muscle. It is about silencing the inner dialogue which is constantly trying to pull us away from the current moment and being still within. It is the act of *Being,* and attuning to the energy which connects *every single thing in existence.* I read a quote recently that stated "We as a people have gone from human *beings* to human *doings."* How very true this is. We have forgotten how to simply be. Doing "nothing" makes us nervous, antsy, and agitated. We feel we must be constantly *doing* something or being productive in some way to the point where we lay awake at night trying to plan out the day ahead before it has even arrived and while we are still exhausted from the previous days activities.

Picture a hawk sitting in a tree. Do you think she is concerned with what she needs to do tomorrow? Where she needs to hunt? How many other hawks are going to be in the area? If that sexy male hawk even noticed her brilliant red tail feathers? Probably not. She simply is. She is existing in the moment, free from fear or worry and hunts, flies, interacts with others, and loves, all in the moment, organically, as the opportunities naturally arise. If she does experience stress or fear, it is because something in her immediate situation is necessitating such a response in order for her survival, such as a larger predator moving into her vicinity, but once the threat is removed or passed, she does not dwell on it, she is back to existing in the moment.

SOULWORK ASSIGNMENT:

Today, I want you to practice meditating, even if only for 10 minutes. Do not think of this as a chore. Think of it as a breath of fresh air. This is your chance to let it all go! Give your mind a rest! All those thoughts that seem so important now will still be there after the 10 minutes are up. There is no need to cling desperately to them. Sit or lay in a comfortable position where you will not be disturbed, close your eyes, and concentrate on your breath. Note the way it feels as it passes through your nostrils, down your throat, into your lungs and belly. Take your time. Go slow. Allow your breath to fill you completely. Hold it for a moment, and then slowly release it, allowing it to flow out of you completely. Feel it, don't think about it. Your only job right now is to BE, to exist, to *breathe*. Just like the trees, just like the flowers, you make the world a more vibrant and beautiful place simply by your existence. It you find yourself thinking about something, thats OK! Simply observe that you are in the process of thinking, and allow the thought to dissipate or float on by, like a cloud over a mountain.

When your 10 minutes are up, you may want to write about your experience in your journal. Did you have any insights or body sensations? Were there certain thoughts that kept popping up? Did you find it easy or difficult to immerse yourself in your breath? Simply record your observations without judgment. They will make a good reference point for you later on down the road.

***Take it a step further: I recommend making meditation a part of your daily self-care routine. If you can set aside 10 to 15 minutes each day for your meditation practice you will experience profound results. You may find that you enjoy it so much you want to extend the time frame to 30 minutes or even an hour. Go for it! Do what feels right for you! I personally like to wake up a little earlier than the rest of my household before the hustle and bustle of the day really kicks in and spend some quiet time in mediation and welcoming the day. For others, a lunch break or right before bed might be the best time to not be disturbed. Tailor your practice to your own unique needs, and you will be much more likely to stick with it.

Day 2- Observing Emotions

Emotions are a product of the mind. They occur when we subconsciously label something as good or bad. Often, the root of the emotion is buried deep within our past experiences, which means that it is very easy for an emotion to pull us away from what is *actually* happening to us. Emotions can be good indicators of whether or not something is "good" or "bad" for us, they can also create frustration when they seemingly take the steering wheel away from you and skid out of control for a not so joyous ride. Many people are unknowingly ruled by their emotions, when in fact, it should be us, as conscious, present, human beings, who are using emotions as a tool to discover who we really are and to connect and engage with our fellow human beings. When we observe our emotions from a new perspective, watching them with curiosity and acceptance rather than passing judgments on them or becoming entangled in their drama, the ego looses it manipulative hold over us and we gain a whole new level of awareness.

Watching your emotions is fairly easy to do, and becomes even easier with time. Eventually it will become second nature, and you will find yourself easily flowing with any and all emotive responses which may be triggered in you, you will use these responses to move about the world in the manner that the authentic self choses to, and not the way of the ego.

The next time you find yourself having an emotionally charged response to something, positive or negative, take a moment to check in with yourself. Ask yourself;
What am I feeling? Happy, sad, nervous? Where am I feeling this emotion in my body? Is it a fluttering in my stomach? A tightening of my throat or tingling behind my knees? How is it affecting my body language? Am I slouching or standing tall? Am I making eye contact? Am I smiling? Then try to pinpoint

what it was that triggered the emotion. Was is a movie you saw? Something someone said? A song you heard or a specific scent? Why do you think this trigger resulted in this emotion?

It may sound like a lot, but you can actually run through your observations very quickly in your mind. If you need to, stop, take a few slow deep breaths, and then begin the observations. When you can answer the last question honestly and without judgment on yourself, you are then able to decide whether or not this particular emotional response is appropriate to the situation, and choose whether or not to act on said emotion.

As an example. I found myself feeling very irritable and offended by the fact that my husband did not respond in the manner I had hoped for when I told him I wanted to start my own business. I had been hoping for a resounding, "That's an awesome idea babe! I know you can do it! You accomplish anything you set your mind to!" What I got was, "Are you sure? How do you know people are going to pay for that? How do you know they even need or want this service? Why do you think it will work for them?"

Well shit. Thanks for believing in me and your unbreakable enthusiasm.

I instantly felt myself getting heated, literally. I could feel my temperature rise, and a tightening in my stomach. My eyebrows came together and my shoulders slumped forward in a cowering and protective posture where I sat. It did not feel good. I asked myself why I was responding in this manner and realized it was because I wanted to have unwavering support from my husband. I asked myself why I needed his support and realized that I didn't, but I wanted it because I was unsure of myself and didn't think I could do it without his support. I asked myself if this were actually the truth and realized it was not. I am the only one responsible for my actions and I cannot blame others for my successes or failures. If I wanted to start my own business, I could. Support would be required from my own self first and foremost. How could I expect anyone else to give me what I was unwilling to give myself? Furthermore, I realized I was responding emotionally to his response because he was giving voice to my inner fears, and asking the very questions I was subconsciously harboring myself. So I took a deep breath, loosened my shoulders as I straightened up, and answered as truthfully as I could, each of his questions. Afterwards, I felt much better about myself for having actually answered the questions I had been afraid to ask myself, and grateful to my husband for having given me the opportunity to face them head on. And after hearing my responses, he became much more encouraging! By choosing to take a moment to observe my emotions rather than letting them take control and saying something like my initial emotional driven response of, "You never support any of my ideas. Do you not think I can do it? Why don't you believe in me?", the whole scenario actually became quite pleasant for all involved.

<u>SOULWORK ASSIGNMENT:</u>

Take some time today to check in with yourself and your body. What are you feeling? Where? Why? Become an explorer of you own inner landscape. Get to know its nooks and crannies. Do not be afraid to lift up the rocks and peek into the dark corners. You will find nothing that you cannot make brighter by flooding it with the light of your awareness. When you are able to observe your emotions and consciously decide how to respond to them, you are able to ask yourself; WWSGD? How would Sensual Goddess respond, how would she use the emotion to her benefit in order to promote even more enjoyment and positivity in her life? Write about your findings in your journal.

Day 3- Body Scanning

Body scanning is great way to re-establish communication with your physical self. All too often we are so busy letting the mind rule our day to day that we begin to ignore the important cues and messages our bodies are trying to communicate with us. How many times do we find ourselves staying up when we are undeniably exhausted, for fear that we will leave some task or assignment undone, that we will not be as productive as we can be? Or overeating to the point of lethargy because we ignore the bodies cues signally to us that we are full? Or we opt for a sugary drink when what the body is really craving is water? Eventually, we may stop hearing the body talk altogether. This is dangerous, as it can easily result in disease. Physical illness and ailments are the bodies way to get our attention. It is the bodies way of shouting at us, a signal that something in our lives is out of balance, and it would behoove the individual to take some time to discover what that something is rather than covering the symptoms up with over-the-counter or prescribed medications.

Sensual Goddess is *very* aware of her body and the signals it sends her on a continuous basis. She has a very intimate relationship with her physical being and is fluent in the unique language of her body. Because of this she is able to circumvent most illness and disease because she immediately knows when something is not serving her bodies greatest good and is able to correct the issue. This in itself is a wonderful benefit to establishing open communication with the body. Whats even more exciting, is that besides avoiding the discomforts of illness, Sensual Goddess is able to actively seek out the sources that *promote* and *increase* her health and vitality. She is not simply surviving. She is thriving. Because of her intimate relationship with her own body, she can experience a much broader and fulfilling spectrum of sensual pleasures and physical delights. She relishes the electrifying touch of skin on skin, or the warm kiss of sunshine on her face. The cool breeze feels like a lovers caress and the experience of eating is a delightful symphony of texture and flavors playing across her tongue. Through her body, she is able to identify those things which serve her greatest potential, and move into them with open arms. The things which are not beneficial to her overall well being, she can gracefully pass on by.

To do a body scan simply sit or lie in a comfortable position where you will not be disturbed. Close your eyes if this helps you focus. Start at your head and work your way down to your feet, taking time to check in with each body part and maybe ask it how it is doing. I know, asking your elbow how it is doing and if there is anything it wants to communicate with you may seem silly, but this is how you are subconsciously programing your self to re-sensitize and attune to the physical cues your body is sending you, cues which may have atrophied over time when your body realized that no matter what it did, you did not listen to it. By consciously giving attention to the various parts of your body, you are re-programming yourself (and body) to say, "Ok. I am here, I am present, and I am listening. What do I need to know in order to experience radiant health and sensuality."

A tight tense spot in the neck may signal a stressful working environment, an ache in the back may be hinting you need a firmer mattress, and a bloated, heavy feeling in the stomach may be asking you to re-evaluate your diet. The cause for a physical cue may be environmental or emotional, (such as a stressful working environment vs. a lumpy mattress), but by not fighting or resisting the cue, simply observing it and allowing yourself to experience it fully, the true cause will usually make itself known. Remember, the body *wants* to be healthy and energetic. This is its natural state of being, so it will respond rapidly and positively to any increase in loving attention.

SOULWORK ASSIGNMENT:

Do a full body scan. Take your time and make it an enjoyable experience. Start at your head and work your way down your body, checking in with your neck, shoulders arms, back, stomach, groin, etc. What sensations do you experience as you focus on each area? Is there a sensation of heat or coolness? A tingling or prickly feeling? Do you feel any pain or pressure? Record your findings in your journal.

Day 4- Identifying the Inner Critic

Ahhh the Inner Critic. We all have one. Its that nasty, judgmental voice
that is constantly telling us we are not thin enough, pretty enough, smart enough, good enough. That nagging voice that seems to pipe up whenever we start feeling too comfortable or confident. "What makes you think this idea will work? How can anyone ever think your body is beautiful and sexy? Why haven't you learned xyz by now, everyone else seems to understand?"

The Inner Critic is the product of our threatened egos, and holds no sway over Sensual Goddess. Sensual Goddess may hear the Inner Critics opinions, but she knows they are not her own, and she lets any negative thoughts or remarks roll off of her as easily as water off of glass. When the Inner Critic realizes his or her judgments are useless, an amazing thing happens; The Critic shuts up. Oh how wonderful it is when you realize you have gone one full day without thinking one negative thought about yourself, or anyone else for that matter! You will feel truly energized and empowered. It may take some time to get to this point, but do not be discouraged. Remember, it is the journey, and not the destination, where the greatest treasures are to be found. We will begin simply by becoming aware of the Inner Critic in the first place.

SOULWORK ASSIGNMENT:

Give your Inner Critic a persona. Maybe it is a cranky old man in judges robes or a snooty prima donna in a business suit. Think of your mind as a holy place, a part of the temple of your body where the Sensual Goddess makes her home. The Inner critic is not welcome here. Anytime you catch this sneaky pest creeping past your threshold, give him a firm boot out the door. Tell him his opinions are not welcome here, dust off your hands, and be done with him. It doesn't matter if you have to do this a hundred times per day. What matters is that you are becoming aware of just how often you let this Inner Critic track its negativity all throughout your psyche. Once you have banished the Critic from your "temple" you can simply get out a mop and broom and clean up his muddy gunk from your interior. (A good way of doing this is to affirm to yourself the exact *opposite* of what the Critic was telling you. "I *am* beautiful. I *am* capable. I *am* enough."

Day 5- Monitoring Thoughts

By now you should be a little more aware of what your internal landscape looks like on a regular basis. You are getting the hang of objectively *feeling* your emotions, and you have identified, and learned to silence, your inner critic.

Today we take it a step further by monitoring our thoughts. Make no mistake, this is powerful stuff! Your reality is the direct result of what you've got going on between the ears. Your environment and the relationships around you offer a brutally honest mirror by which to observe your own mental state of being. As within, so without. If you are unhappy, you are responsible. If you are joyful and content, you are responsible. And you always have the capability to change, for the better or worse. Many of the conflicts and issues we face as a modern society are the direct result of *individuals*, (yes, that means you and I!), not taking responsibility for their thoughts. This, for the most part, is not done intentionally. Many of us have never been taught skills such as meditation, we are not aware of the awesome POWER contained in our minds, we are not even conscious of the majority of our internal chatter on a daily basis. I once read a statistic that claimed on average, 95% of what a person thinks each day is repetitive, and of that, about 85% is negative! Holy sheet! You may be thinking, (as I did when I first read this), that these numbers sound a little extreme and couldn't possible apply to you. "No way!" I thought, "I am not a negative person! I am so full of sunshine and rainbows...." and then, just to prove myself right, I began to check in with my own thoughts more frequently throughout the day. I was aghast by what I discovered: The statistic was scary accurate! For one, most of what I was thinking was indeed very repetitive. Usually I would return to the same thoughts over and over again even over the course of one hour. Thoughts like "I need to pay the upcoming bills, I should be working out, I should eat healthier food, In a few hours my daughter will need a nap, I need to clean the house, what will we have for dinner, what time is it, how much longer until my husband gets home, I need to start the laundry…" and on and on and on. I had an endless to do list on repeat in my head, a mild, yet constant, source of stress. Furthermore, I was astounded at how much of what I thought was not very pleasant. I criticized myself viciously, (Ugh, why am I breaking out again? Did I gain weight? Why haven't I washed the dishes? I am a shitty housekeeper!), I silently criticized other people, the way they looked or acted, I mentally attacked drivers on the road, cursed long lines in the grocery store, bemoaned southern California traffic, became frustrated when watching the news or listening to the radio, and wanted to pull my hair out each time I scrolled through my Facebook newsfeed. I was definitely not as zen as I had originally considered myself to be. All this changed when I learned how to bear witness to my mind, in a loving and accepting way. Little by little, I was able to clear out my mental junk and free up a vast amount of energy for more pleasant pursuits. Now it's time for you to experiment with this as well. It does take a little practice, but is not particularly difficult.

SOULWORK ASSIGNMENT:

Become a witness to your thoughts. This is actually the easy part. The hard part is remembering to check in with yourself! But with practice, it becomes automatic, and any thought that is not serving your greatest good will light up like a red flag, at which point it can be easily dealt with or transformed into a positive thought.

To begin, simply take a deep breath, and take a moment to observe what you are thinking from an *outside* perspective. Just observe. Do not pass judgments or criticize yourself for what you find. Recognize that you are *not* your thoughts, (just as you are *not* your emotions), and that much of what we think on a daily basis is the direct result of a lifetime of unconscious programming drilled into us by our parents, our peers, our communities, and the media. Find joy and excitement in the fact that now, as a sensually awake and mature adult, you are the one who gets to be in charge of the stories that play out in your head. YOU are the sole gatekeeper of your beautiful mind.

Become your own witness. You may feel a little strange at first, watching your thoughts objectively as opposed to being completely immersed in them and consumed by their content, but pretend you are your own counselor, best friend, or fairy godmother. As such, your first job is simply to *listen*, to become aware of the state of things as interpreted by you, with acceptance, love, and an open heart and mind. Remember to check in and "watch" your thoughts several times throughout the day, particularly if you are feeling stressed out or low on energy. See if you can find any patterns or correlations. Have fun with it! Be a detective/ explorer of your own personal jungle. Record your findings in your journal.

Day 6- Connecting With the Breath

Breath is life. Breath is what intimately connects us to one another and to all living things in existence. The air we breath has been breathed many times before, by those across the planet, by our ancestors, by the dinosaurs and the insects and the wild horses thundering across the plains. We breathe each other in, and we breath each other out. The act of breathing is an interdependent dance of cooperation between us and the planet we are a part of; We breath the oxygen released by the oceans and the forests, we breath out the carbon dioxide the trees and oceans need for survival, and the cycle repeats. We are ALL connected by breath, no matter how you look at it. When there is no breath, there is no life. Breathing is also one of the most sensual acts you can experience, and what luck that it is something we must do regularly throughout the day! A full deep breath brings oxygen and Prana (life-force) to each and every cell in our body. It makes our blood rich and nutrient dense and stimulates our root chakra and sex organs as our diaphragm expands out down, giving us an internal massage and increasing blood flow and sensitivity in the genitals. Breathing properly leads to glowing skin, a superhuman immune system, full body orgasms, and more. Unfortunately, many of us do not know how to breathe properly. A large part of this stems from the harsh ways in which babies are born in our culture. Newborns are taken from their mothers and their cords are cut before they have even had the time to clear all the amniotic fluid from their lungs. As a result, the first breath is painful and full of fear and confusion. Many of us do not recover fully from this and spend the rest of our lives afraid to breathe to our full capacity for a subconscious fear of inducing pain.

Even if we were born in a gentle manner, our fast paced and overstimulated lives are much more conducive to short, quick breathing than to long, full, deep breaths. We go throughout the day breathing fast and shallow and even if we feel "normal" this breathing pattern tells our bodies that we are in a constant state of stress. It is a "flight or fight" breath, and it is not the healthiest way to partake in this life's magical act of breathing.

A buddhist monk has been quoted as stating that if a person becomes aware of each breath they are taking, if only for one day, that person will reach enlightenment. All yoga, tantra, and many ancient religions focus attention on the art of breathing. The power contained within conscious breathing has been known, kept, and shared for centuries. You too, can easily partake in this radiant practice.

SOULWORK ASSIGNMENT:

Your assignment today is simply to become aware of your breath. Thats it. As many times today as you can. Take note of your first conscious breath after waking. The way you breathe in the shower, when you are driving, when you are eating, when you are speaking or listening. Just give it your attention. You will notice that with your attention, your breath automatically deepens and slows. This is the normal breath pattern of a person in a relaxed state of being, the state that is most conductive to health and sensuality. You do not have to close your eyes or meditate if you do not feel like it, but take some time experiencing the sensation of taking as much air into your body as possible, holding it a moment, and then releasing fully. Breathe into your diaphragm, so that your stomach expands out, and your chest rises. Let your self feel the oxygen bringing life to each perfect cell in your body, healing and rejuvenating.

Day 7- Learning to Just Be

We have gone from a species of human BEINGS to a species of human DOERS. Being still and silent makes us agitated and uncomfortable. Going slow sends our stress levels soaring. Just take a look around at all the people on their cell phones as they wait for their coffee or stand in line at the grocery store. Take note whether or not you regularly allow yourself to relax. I mean *really* relax, without thinking about what needs to get done in the near future or what you should be doing instead. I have found that in my own experience and also in working with my clients that even when we are able to give ourselves permission to relax, we are still in a "doers" mind set. We schedule in relaxation as something that should get done,and have a set of activities that are appropriate enough to fall into that category, such as reading a book, watching a movie, knitting a scarf or watering the garden, all of which are fine and dandy, but how comfortable are you actually doing nothing? Simply *BEING*. With nothing on your agenda but breathing in and out. Existing. Your existence in and of itself is such a beautiful and awe inspiring miracle, how often do you really let yourself just revel in being alive and aware?

SOULWORK ASSIGNMENT:

At some point today, give yourself permission to just BE. Take a lesson from a tree or your favorite wildflower. Notice how they stand true and tall, exposed and open to the elements, unafraid of life, and with no need to go anywhere, do anything, or be anything other than what they are at that given moment. See how they witness the world around them, note how effortlessly they are a part of nature and the landscape around them. Your only job here and now is to exist, to breath, to feel alive. There is nothing else you need to worry or think about. Give yourself permission to let it all go. Feel the wind on your face, the sunshine on your skin, see the rainbow of colors that envelops you, and do *nothing*.

WEEK 2: AWAKENING THE SENSES

Congratulations! You have made it to the second week! This is no small feat as many find the introspective nature of week one a bit daunting and uncomfortable. This is totally normal and a natural response to unfamiliarity. But take heart! You are well on your way to becoming the Sensual Goddess you know you are meant to be! (Hint: YOU ALREADY ARE! We are just clearing the debris from body mind and spirit which are inhibiting you from realizing this!). This will be a fun filled week. Here is where we really get to begin exploring the physical juiciness that is the lifeblood of any Sensual Goddess. Sensuality is a celebration of our bodies and our senses. Our senses are what enable us to navigate the world around us. They warn us of danger, steer us from pain, and also allow us the opportunity to experience an infinite capacity of pleasure, beauty, and joy. They are a Sensual Goddess' best friend, and in her, they are sharp and finely tuned extensions of herself. She uses them to pursue her desires, and shape the world around her into a playground for her body and spirit.

For most of us, our senses have been severely dulled. This is a result of overstimulation, pollutants in our environments, (light pollution, noise pollution, air pollution, artificial flavoring agents, to name a few), and a general lack of awareness. We are so used to depending on everyone outside of ourselves to take care of our most basic needs, that we forget to exercise our own amazing senses, and with neglect they can begin to atrophy. But luckily, it is very easy, and *fun,* to begin to reawaken our sensual potential. As they begin to come alive, you will begin to experience life in a whole new and exciting way. Colors will be brighter, food will be tastier, music will be more enchanting, smells will be sweeter, and each caress against your skin will seem more luxurious than ever before. Much of what you will be learning from here on out will piggy back or build on what you have learned in the previous week. Enjoy this next chapter of assignments, you Sensual Woman you!

Day 8- Colors and Light

Oh the beauty of sight! Our eyes, the windows to our souls, bless us by allowing our spirits to peer out of the temples of our bodies and gaze in awe at the world around us. DO NOT take your vision for granted! (Just ask anyone with failing vision or who lives with blindness). Allow the beautiful things around you to stimulate and excite you. Be inspired. Be humbled. Be awestruck. Allow your gaze to travel to places it is not used to going, such as into the distance. We are so used to having everything right around us, within our immediate vicinity, that we rarely have to gaze farther than our computer screen, the walls of our house, or past the bumper of the car in front of us. Let your eye muscles stretch to the horizon. Observe the contours of a distant mountain range, the slow evolution of a cumulous cloud. Or watch the way the sunlight dances through the leaves of trees and speckles the ground beneath. REALLY take in the beauty of each unique face of the people around you. Do they look happy or sad? Are they young or old? What is there style of dress or posture? There is so much to see! Look for tiny spherical dew drops sparkling on emerald blades of grass. Admire the bright sheen on a newly washed car. Delight in the soft plumpness of your toddlers rosy cheek. Wherever you look, find the beauty, find the mystery. Do not strain your eyes with too much artificial light. Watch the sunrise and sunset if you can, (try connecting with your breath, as in week one, as you do so!). When the sun goes down, experiment with lighting your home with candles or a softer than normal light source. If you have a desk job, make sure you look up from your screen every few moments and find something to admire in the distance, to properly exercise your iris. If you find yourself waiting for something, and automatically reaching for your phone for a quick distraction, resit the urge and practice todays Soulwork assignment instead.

SOULWORK ASSIGNEMNT:

Find the rainbow. At any given time throughout the day, and as many times as you like, look around your environment for all the colors on the spectrum. Look for reds, then oranges, then yellows, and find as many things of each color as you can until you have found all the colors in the rainbow! Write them down in your journal if you like. If you are really feeling visually inspired, start observing different shadows and light patterns, as well as the *empty* space created by the structures around you. This will pull you into the present moment and get your sensual creative juices flowing! Bonus points if you can sketch, (yes, even poorly!) your observations.

Day 9- Learning to Listen

A baby laughing. Birds chirping. Rain falling. A lovers sigh. A friends welcomed greeting. A flamenco dancers feet tapping a fast rhythm to an even faster guitar. What sounds do you love? What sounds do you hear on a daily basis? Are you even aware of them? Do you know what a squirrels excited chirp sounds like? Or can you tell which direction the wind is coming from by the way it rustles through the trees? Do you let yourself hear the waves of the ocean or the power of your breath as you jog along the boardwalk, or do you religiously plug into your favorite playlist when out in nature? The universe is constantly speaking to you, Sensual Woman. Learn how to listen and it will begin to SING the most beautiful song you have ever heard!

SOULWORK ASSIGNMENT:

Just listen. Wherever you happen to be. Close your eyes if it helps, and see if you can identify all the different sounds that come to you. Airplanes, traffic, dogs barking, neighbors laughing, high heels on tile, your own heart beat, your *deep steady breathing*. Observe what you hear and refrain from labeling the sounds as good or bad. Let them pass through you. Soak in their vibrations. Write your findings in your journal. You may notice you can easily identify sounds you weren't even aware were present in your neighborhood!

Day 10- An Exploration of Scent

Scent holds a special power for us. It can be extremely nostalgic, (one sniff of apple blossoms and you are a child again running carefree through your grandmothers orchard), and overwhelmingly seductive. Why do you think the perfume business is a multi*billion* dollar industry? Scented candles? Air fresheners?

Certain scents have even been shown to have beneficial effects on our minds. Studies have supported the notion of the calming effects of lavender, or the naturally invigorating smell of fresh citrus. Mint makes one more focused, cedar makes us grounded and peaceful, and roses and jasmine leave us feeling romantic and sensitive.

A Sensual Goddess is well aware of the magical effects of scent. She uses it while she cooks, eats, bathes, and plays. She uses natural incense and essential oils to flavor the atmosphere with her latest bliss seeking whims. She always has time to stop and smell the roses, and pine trees, and coffee. and fresh herbal teas.

SOULWORK ASSIGNMENT:

Go on a scent safari!*** Start in your home. What delicious smells are hidden here? Open the spice cabinet. Can you identify all your spices and herbs by scent alone? What are you drinking? Does your water have a certain smell? What about the carrots you snack on. Fresh laundry, artisan soap bars, and fresh cut flowers are all waiting to be appreciated. Go for a walk around the block and pay attention to what you smell. Wet earth. Gasoline. Pine. A nearby bakery. Go to the produce section of you local farmers market and breath deep! Smell each piece of fruit of vegetable as if you were experiencing it for the first time. As you cook your meals, let your nose delight in the scrumptious aromas your culinary creations emit, no matter if they are simplistic or complex. In your journal, write down any scents you associate with the different seasons, (pine and hot chocolate in the winter, wildflowers and rain in the spring time, sunscreen and salt water in the summer, pumpkin pie and spiced lattes in the fall…). Then go seek out your favorites.

***Many (I would argue most) products we buy specifically for scent or that are scented as an added bonus (such as dish soap, tampons, or laundry detergent), use toxic chemicals to achieve the desirable smell. This includes everything from perfume and body washes, to candles and incense. Please try to avoid these at all costs. Breathing in toxins is harmful to your health. Take time to read labels and to seek out naturally occurring beautiful smells and products that use only natural ingredients. You will not have to look far, and the results will be much more beneficial.

Day 11- Taste and Sensual Eating

Eating is one of the most sensual and sexy acts we can experience. It gives us life, sustains us, and can be *immensely* pleasurable. Don't believe me? Just watch, (or better yet READ), "Like Water for Chocolate". Yet just as in sex, so much of us rush through our meals, seeking only the end result- to fill our bellies immediately, that we miss out on so many of the sensory pleasures eating offers us.

Sensual Goddess knows of the bliss contained in the act of eating, and she utilizes it fully. She eats slowly and consciously and savors each bite. She eats with all of her senses, allowing her self to enjoy the appearance of a well prepared meal, the savory scents, the sound of the food sizzling on the stove. She takes in the textures, and is never afraid to eat with her hands. She chews slowly, allowing herself to appreciate the dance of flavors, and always chews her food completely before swallowing. She is grateful and appreciative of each and everything she takes into her body. She recognizes that food is life, and that life is good. In fact, it is wondrous.

SOULWORK ASSIGNMENT:

If you are not in the habit of eating slowly and fully appreciating each meal, now is the time to start. Start with just one meal, even if that means you need to wake up a full 30 minutes earlier to enjoy your bowl of cereal in peace. Bonus points if you are able to cook a meal at home, and turn the cooking process into a sexy exploration of the senses as well. Light a candle, take off your bra, put on some soothing music, and have fun with it!

Day 12- The Joy of Touch

Our skin is the largest organ on our bodies. It protects us, contains us, and enables us to experience the warning signs of pain, as well as sweet, sweet decadent pleasure. It also gives us clues as to how healthy our insides are looking. Clear, radiant skin is a sure sign of health just as dry or irritated skin is a symptom of something in our self-care routine needing adjustment. Sensual Goddess delights in her skin. She loves and nurtures it. She does not smother it with harsh chemicals or pick and prod at its imperfections. She listens to what her skin is telling her. If it is dry, she lovingly rubs it with coconut oil or natural lotions. If it is irritated, she does not attempt to cover up the symptoms but rather takes some time to communicate with her body and address the cause.

She loves the feel of sunlight on bare shoulders as much as she delights in a fresh cold breeze against her cheeks. Of course, one of the things she loves the most about her skin is the feeling of loving hands or a loving body caressing every inch of it. Sometimes these hands belong to a special lover, other times, they are her own. Either way, she finds immense enjoyment from the sensations her skin allows her to experience.

SOULWORK ASSIGNMENT:

In your Sensual Goddess Diary, take some time to make a list of all the things you can think of that feel good against your skin. Warm beach sand, a feather, fresh green grass, silk panties, a soft new makeup brush, a favorite sweater, your child's bare cheek, your cats soft fur, summer rain, or a cool quartz crystal. You get the idea. You can let your imagination run wild here. For example, maybe you've never experienced what it feels like to sink into a mud bath, but if it's something that sounds luxurious and pleasurable to you, write it down.

Next, see how many touchy feely delights you can bestow upon you radiant skin throughout the day. Run a flower petal along your cheek bone. Put on your favorite cozy socks. Wear your favorite silk blouse over your bare chest. Take your time rubbing warm coconut oil over every inch of your body. *Every inch!* Sunbathe naked!!! Press your lips against the skin of a peach or ask someone close to you for a gentle shoulder rub. Don't be shy! At the end of the day write about your experiences and take note of the ones you and your skin loved the most.

***Note: One of the best things a Goddess can do for her skin (and health in general), besides avoiding harsh chemicals, is to make sure she is drinking plenty of water. It is extremely important to stay well hydrated, especially if you want beautiful, dewy, glowing skin, which is your birthright lady!

Day 13- Grounding

You may notice that as you expand your capacity for experiencing the world through your senses, other senses begin to develop as well, such as your intuition and ability to sense various forms of energy, negative or positive. This is nothing to be alarmed about. All people are naturally intuitive, and women are exceptionally so. Most of us have learned from a young age to ignore our intuition in favor of reason and logic, but Sensual Goddess knows that her intuition and energetic sensitivity is one of her greatest tools for moving through the world and responding to her environment with joy, love, and compassion.

Whether or not you feel like your intuition is speaking loud and clear to you or is still finding its voice, it is important to recognize that your physical and energetic body (your aura), do indeed pick up various forms of energy throughout the day. Some if this energy is good and invigorating, helping us to be the vibrant glowing women we know we truly are, but other energy is draining and depleting. Left unattended it can accumulate like dust over an otherwise clear window, or clutter the aura with energetic debris that can create blockages and inhibit our ability to live sensually and freely. Grounding is an important practice for anyone who is practicing spiritual development or who is simply wanting to feel more present and centered in their bodies, (In fact, I would argue that it-along with meditation- is a very important and beneficial practice to *all* people everywhere!). Grounding literally means connecting to the energy of the earth, recognizing that we are a part of nature, and not apart from nature, and allowing the healing energies of the earth below us to absorb and neutralize any negative or unwanted energy or vibrations we pick up as we go about our day to day lives.

Grounding provides for a clear and healthy flow of energy, communication with our bodies and with others, and a new level of personal control, or sovereignty, as I like to think of it. It provides not only connection, but a foundation and release system for all unwanted energies. When we are not grounded, it is easy to feel out of control, out of touch with reality, disconnected from your physicality, and easily frightened or disturbed. These are not attributes we wish to cultivate with our Sensual Goddess, and so I encourage you to make a sincere effort to incorporate grounding into part of your regular self care routine.

www.healingforgrounding.com states that one of the many important benefits from grounding is:

"Pleasure, joy, and ecstasy: related to life force- the state of joy and pleasure is a natural one, and our birthright. The very sensation of pleasure requires us to be embodied; connecting deeper into our bodies (ie, grounding deeper) opens up the channels for us to feel more of life's richness."

If that isn't part of the Sensual Goddess' MO I don't know what is! I promise you it will be worth the little effort it takes to practice this beautiful technique!

SOULWORK ASSIGNMENT:

Get grounded! Grounding is simple to do and actually can be immensely enjoyable. And there are various ways to accomplish it! One of the most common is to sit or stand in a relaxed state with the eyes closed and imagine tree roots growing out of your feet or the base of your spine and sinking deep into the center of the earth, connecting you to all the energies and life forces contained within. From here you can both draw up these rich energies or send down into the earth that which is not serving your greatest good, such as any anger, fear, physical tension, or apprehension. The earth takes these energies and recycles them into a more vibrant life force essence, much in the way she creates life giving fertilizer out of death and decay. This technique works wonderfully, however, for our sensual purposes this week, I suggest you try some of the other, more body led, (as opposed to mental), techniques. As always, do what speaks to you and what feel good. Let your senses and your intuition be your guide. Some of my favorite techniques for grounding are as follows:

*Go for a walk in nature. Bare foot is best. Try walking along the seashore or across a grassy field.

*Hug a tree. Really!

*Eat a local and seasonal meal of roots, legumes, and other veggies if you like.

*Take an epsom salt bath.

*Take a break from the computer and social media.

*Diffuse oils or burn incense that remind you of the earth, such as pine, cedar wood, sage, or rosemary.

*Carry a crystal or favorite stone. Hematite is famed for it's natural grounding properties.

*Simply go outside. Garden, walk, dance, use all 5 of the senses we have been working on enhancing to take in and fully experience your surroundings, or just sit and breath in the fresh air.

*Dig a hole in the dirt and fill it with water. When its good and muddy, sink your feet in and feel the squish between your toes. Smile and laugh.

Write about your grounding experiences in your Sensual Goddess Diary.

Day 14- Singing and Being heard

As girls, many of us are taught, whether actively or passively, to been seen and not heard. To not speak unless spoken to. To be silent rather than say something that may cause others to feel uncomfortable. Sometimes, as we ran around in our innocence, laughing, yelling, and singing just for the joy of it, we were told to be quite, because this noise we were making was a nuisance to our tired parents, the neighbors, our classmates. In short we were taught to quiet our voices for the sake of those around us. Soon we also learned what things were ok to speak about and what was taboo. We were taught that to speak of our feelings was embarrassing, to voice our pride and awareness at our budding sexuality was shameful, to speak of things that could be felt but not seen was considered crazy, and to voice opinions different from the norm was opening up the door for judgment and social ostracization.

As adults, many of these rules still apply, and then some. For many, it is difficult to voice our opinions and feelings, be they good or bad, out of fear of what the listener will think. Too often "I love you's" go unspoken because the timing is deemed inappropriate or because we are not used to saying it or the recipient not used to hearing it. Too often we bite our tongues when something someone says or does makes us angry or when we disagree with what is being said, for fear of creating conflict and inviting criticism. Too often we swallow the natural sounds of pleasure that want to rise up out of us from our core, be they from eating, deep relaxation, or making love, because again, our sensual pleasure is something to be ashamed and embarrassed of. What will the neighbors think if they hear you moaning in ecstasy as you make love? What will the in-laws think if you groan your delight while eating a well-appreciated meal? Not very lady-like is it? Well guess what- Sensual Goddess doesn't give a hoot about being lady-like.

We may have been raised in a culture that praises us for our silence, but Sensual Goddess challenges us to recognize when these habits are no longer serving our greatest good and are actually inhibiting our sensual expression. She urges us to break free of this conditioning and to take back the power of your voice. Speak up! Sing! Be comfortable being heard! The voice of a Sensual Goddess is a true gift, both in expressing and creating pleasure and delight. She is the one who sings to the woodland creatures in the forest, (or to herself in the shower, regardless of who might hear), she is the one who does not swallow her laughter, but lets it pour forth with a childlike abandon. She speaks her mind and is not afraid to give praise or voice dissent, (nor is she afraid of receiving criticism for the things she says, as her words are chosen carefully and she is confident in her ideals and values). Her voice is a great tool and guide when making love, and she does not silence it here either. She lets her partner know exactly what she wants and when she wants it. She demonstrates with her sighs, squeals, moans and groans, what she likes and how she likes it. The sounds she creates in the act of lovemaking hold their own delicious energy and serve to heighten the experience both for her and for her lover.

I admit, on my own quest for Sensual Awakening, using my voice and especially being heard was one of the most uncomfortable hurdles I had to overcome. But once I broke through that barrier, a whole new arena of delight opened up for me. One of the most helpful tools I used to overcome this was song. Singing! Singing feels sooo wonderful! Ask any small child. I love the way children sing at the top of their lungs, without inhibition simply because it makes them feel good. They don't care if they are on key or not. For most adults however, (and again, I find this especially true for women), if we are not told from a young age that we are going to be the next American Idol, this natural confidence fades, and we cringe at the thought of having to sing, or even speak, in public. Even if Sensual Goddess was not meant to be the next pop super-star, even if her voice is not reminiscent of angels singing praises, she still uses it, and enjoys doing so!

SOULWORK ASSIGNMENT:

Sing! And if you are not there yet, work up to singing in front of other people. You don't have to belt anything out at the top of your lungs, singing along softly to a song on the radio will suffice, but if you want to shout it out, go right ahead!

If this idea makes your stomach knot, as it did mine, start small and in private.

You can sing loudly while driving in your car, hum softly while cooking dinner, or turn up your favorite track loud enough that you can sing along to it at a comfortable volume without feeling like you are on center stage. Don't worry, Sensual

Goddess has no problem being on center stage, and with practice, you will embody this confidence as well. For now, just keep practicing using your voice in ways that you are unused to. You will soon discover how delightful this feels to you and your soul and naturally bloom into a woman who has no problem being heard in the world.

WEEK 3: AWAKENING THE GODDESS

Welcome to week three, and one of my personal favorites when it comes to this five week long course! This is where things start to get really fun and creativity begins to really blossom. This is the week where *you* start to earnestly embrace what it means to act and think like your inner Sensual Goddess. In other words, like your true authentic self. There are few things as gratifying as beginning to recognize and come home to yourself, to reconnect to your soul and what makes it sing. I hope you find this week as magical as I do. Enjoy!

Day 15- Create a Sensual Shrine

The first day of the third week of the course! Three has always been recognized as a mystical number and we ring in the first day of the third transformative week with a momentous activity. Today we bring the first physical manifestations of our inner Goddess into our day to day lives by giving her a proper place in our homes and welcoming her into our real world environments.

It is important that Sensual Goddess has a place to call her own. The ideal place of course, is within your body and your heart, and indeed, she does already dwell there, though she may be struggling for a way to express herself. That is why, until we are proficient at fully embodying and expressing her spirit as our own as easily and effortlessly as one and the same, it is immensely helpful to set aside a special place where her energy can be readily seen and felt by you on a regular basis, so that the two of you may get acquainted with each other and you can learn to feel what the Sensual energy of you inner Goddess feels like. It also gives you a sacred place to mediate, dream, contemplate, find inspiration, and create. More importantly, it is a place where you honor _you_ and the beautiful, unique, sexy and seductive woman you are. It is a place, physically and emotionally, where you learn to love, appreciate, respect, and be kind to yourself, through the bond you share with your inner Goddess.

SOULWORK ASSIGNMENT:

Set aside a place in your home and turn it into your own personal Sensual Shrine. This can be on a shelf, a desk, or even a kitchen or bathroom counter. I've even seen beautiful shrines created on windowsills or in closets! Your shrine can be as big or small, simple or elaborate as you like. Some women feel more comfortable placing a small statue and crystal on the windowsill whilst others hang a framed piece of seductive artwork over the mantle which they then drape with silk and candles, adorn with voluptuous female figurines and phallus like sculptures, and vases of roses, all right smack dab in the middle of their living room, (which I LOVE by the way!)

The important thing is to make your shrine suited to *you* and what turns you on. You can use pictures, flowers, crystals, statues, incense, or sensual poetry you have copied onto pretty stationary. Feathers, shells, your Sensual Goddess Diary, and any and all representations of the sacred yoni or the moon are also always a lovely idea. But really, you can make it anyway you like, because it is yours and yours alone, and unique to you and your wild spirit. The only suggestions I really encourage you to stick to are placing it in an area where you will be able to see and connect with it on a daily basis, and to have it in a place where it is easily accessible so that you can take away and add to it as your tastes and preferences fluctuate. Also it is advantageous to have it somewhere where you can easily relax in front of it or with your shrine in full view, so that you can contemplate and absorb its many juicy facets and perhaps meditate on its beauty and inspirational energies if you feel inspired to do so.

Day 16- Say Yes to Pleasure

So often we skirt away from our own pleasure, denying ourselves the joy of what our body, minds, and spirits really crave. Our culture tends to create an aura of shame around our desires, especially if they are sexual. But this goes for many other aspects of our daily lives as well. Often times, we are our own worst pleasure police. If we do allow ourselves to do something we really enjoy, it is many times tinged with a sense of guilt or embarrassment. Can we really enjoy that extra cookie without mentally kicking ourselves for it? Can we take time out of our busy lives to cultivate some quite space and alone time without feeling guilty because we should be spending time with the kids or husband or partner? Can we decide to spend an hour painting or sewing or reading instead of tackling that never-ending list of household chores, and not feel bad about it? Your Sensual Goddess assures you, Yes! You can! And furthermore, you deserve to! We each have this one life to live, and Sensual Goddess is determined to experience as much bliss filled joy during it as possible. Saying yes to pleasure does not mean you are being irresponsible. It means you are really listening to your body and your soul, and giving them what they need in order to thrive, shine, and feel wonderfully and wildly alive.

SOULWORK ASSIGNMENT:

Give yourself permission to say "YES" to yourself when you would normally say no. As many times today as possible. Do you want to wear your sexy high heels to work when you would normally opt for the pair you have labeled "office appropriate"? Do it. Are you craving an ice cream sundae from the new creamery down the street even though it doesn't fit with your diet plans? Get one, and enjoy it guilt free! Buy yourself that pretty necklace you have been eyeballing, or treat yourself to the pedicure or massage you keep saying you are going to get but never do. Go for a nice long walk outside instead of going to the gym, take a luxurious epsom salt bath instead of doing the dishes. Read an indulgent romance novel. Turn up your favorite tunes and dance around the house in your favorite lingerie, or buy/ forage yourself a beautiful bouquet of flowers. And if you find yourself making love and wanting to tell your partner to do this or that, or to keep doing whatever they are doing, but usually stay silent or passive, speak up! Take the lead! Enjoy the thrill of taking control of your own ecstatic experience! Get used to giving yourself what you want and doing what you want without feeling like you are doing something wrong. Sensual Goddess never feels guilty for treating herself like the queen she is!

Day 17- Creating Pleasure

Ok, so yesterday you got used to the idea of saying yes to pleasure. Good work! Today we are going to work on *creating* pleasure, which is one of the many useful skills you will hone and sharpen as you learn to embrace your inner Goddess fully.

The reality is, even though most of us have *plenty* of room for accepting more pleasurable experiences into our lives on a daily basis, we also have responsibilities that need our constant attention. Jobs, households, children, relationships. The list goes on. The wonderful thing about making friends with Sensual Goddess is that she is able to bring a sense of delight and sensuality to whatever it is she is doing. If she finds that she is not enjoying something that must be done, she uses her creativity to make it more enjoyable for herself. She is an expert at finding ways to squeeze pleasure out of the most mundane and un-stimulating tasks. When you follow her lead this becomes second nature, and you will find that your mental space shifts from one of negativity to positivity easily and naturally. You will begin to readily see the glass as half full, to see the gift or lesson in every situation. To recognize and appreciate the miracle of life and your own brilliant and vibrant existence, no matter where you are or what you are doing. You will glow from the inside out, with confidence, gratitude, and grace. Furthermore, you will discover that it is *fun* to find the silver lining. It is a form of creativity and art to make something beautiful and enjoyable out of that which is not. This is an exercise in alchemy, where you get to create gold out of base material.

SOULWORK ASSIGNMENT:

Pick something today that you must get done but are not particularly looking forward to doing. Is it driving your long commute to work? Sitting at a desk all day? Cooking dinner? Doing the dishes? Tending to a sick child? Whatever it is, think of a way to make it more enjoyable. You don't have to turn it into something spectacular. I admit, it may be hard, especially in the beginning, to really get excited over the idea of cleaning the guest bathroom, but the idea is to make it *more* enjoyable than it would normally be for you, even if only by a little bit. And with practice, who knows, you may be eagerly rolling up your sleeves and grabbing the toilet brush in anticipation of a half hour of listening to your favorite podcast while inhaling your most delicious essential oil blend which you diffuse during the scrubbing process and then allowing your feet to soak in your newly cleaned bathtub as you add a few rose petals to the steamy water and meditate on how nice it feels to relax in a fresh sparkling bathroom.

If it is a long commute you are dreading, pick an audiobook or interesting podcast to listen to and brew a thermos of your favorite tea or beverage to sip on as you inch along. Or put on your favorite album and take the opportunity to sing freely at the top of your lungs all the way to work. If the idea of sitting at a desk all day long makes you shudder, see if you can replace your office chair with a yoga ball. You can also look up different stretches or poses to do in your chair and set an alarm or timer so that you take a break every 30mins or hour to do a quick, unobtrusive routine. You can also get up to stretch or walk around for a few minutes. Most workplaces will not object to this as good health and movement has been shown to increase concentration and productivity. Also, make your desk an inviting place. Place a live plant, a crystal, a photograph of a loved one or scene from nature, or a favorite quote or affirmation where it is easily visible. Every so often, divert your eyes away from your computer screen and look either out the window, or at your photo/affirmation, whatever it may be. Give your eyes a break and take in the energy of the scene or words you have chosen.

Use the same sense of play and creativity no matter what "chore" you are tackling. Go easy on yourself, don't expect to immediately jump for joy at the idea of doing the dishes, but acknowledge the fact that you are doing something for yourself solely because you deserve to make the experience as pleasant as possible, even if it is as simple as lighting an incense, putting on some soothing music, and selecting the most delicious smelling dish soap you can find. Make it your playful mission to squeeze as much joy out of mundane, everyday task as you can. Write about your experience in your Goddess Diary.

Day 18- Being Grateful

A big part of the Sensual Goddess attitude is gratitude. When you are consciously grateful for the many blessings that are present in your life, three things happen almost immediately.

1. Like the domino effect, once you get in the habit of noticing the big things you are grateful for, you begin to notice more and more things to feel good about.
2. This enlivens and invigorates your sense of sensuality, as you can more fully appreciate the sound of the wind through the leaves, the warmth of sunlight on your skin, the feel of your softest blanket against your naked body, the smell of fresh baked bread as you walk by a local bakery.
3. This serves to make you more present in the current moment, the surprisingly elusive "Now", and as a result, you almost always experience a greater sense of peace,

happiness and joy, right in the here and now. The present moment becomes a delicious gift.

*** As a bonus, you will often find that once you have adopted this attitude of gratitude, many more wonderful things begin happening to you and around you that you can be grateful for! It is as if the Universe suddenly begins to conspire to give you exactly what you want, (though of course, we know that the Universe is *always* conspiring to give us what we want, and that it is up to us to be conscious and open enough to be able to receive these gifts.) I love the way my mother explains it; "If I give someone a gift, and they take it without a thank you or any authentic show of appreciation, I am less inclined to go out of my way to do something nice for that person in the future. But if I give a gift and the recipient is genuinely appreciative and thankful, if I can see that I've made them happy and that they appreciate the effort I've made on their behalf, it makes me feel good. It makes me want to keep doing nice things for that person. I think the Universe works in much the same way."

SOULWORK ASSIGNMENT:

Keep a gratitude journal. You may have heard of this practice before, it is quite popular, but that is because it is so effective! It is a simple way to become aware of and consciously acknowledge your blessings. In addition, it gets you in the habit of thinking positive, and in seeing the glass as half full, which is the usual mentality of the Sensual Goddess.

To begin, pick out a pretty notebook or journal separate from your Goddess Diary, (you may use your Goddess Diary if you want, but I find it better to have a separate Gratitude Journal that way if you are feeling blue or simply wanting a pick me up, you can flip through your gratitude journal to see all the ways you are blessed without having to search through other content). Every morning, or every night before bed, (or both if you want!), get in the habit of listing at least 5 things you are grateful for. You can also make your list as long as you want. If you are not in a good space mentally or emotionally and are feeling stuck, start with the basics. Did you wake up this morning? (Thats always something to be grateful for!) Do you have a home or apartment? A roof over your head. Do you have access to drinking water and food on a regular basis? Do you have cloths to wear and keep you comfortable in the elements? Do you have a vehicle? Are you literate? Do you live in a conflict free zone where you don't have to worry about being bombed or abducted. It sounds dramatic, but if you answered yes to these questions, that puts you in the elite. You are within the top 2% of the global population, many who lack the basic necessities to live out healthy and comfortable lives. That makes you and I very blessed indeed.

You can also be thankful for the little things, like hearing your favorite song on the radio, receiving a smile from a stranger, smelling a fresh rainfall, taking a hot shower, or enjoying a cup of coffee. When it comes to feeling gratitude, don't limit yourself!

Day 19- Saying No without Guilt

Women are natural nurturers and givers. That is part of what makes us so wonderful and magical. Unfortunately, todays demanding and fast paced society makes it so that often we are giving to everyone else but ourselves. We feel obligated to fill so many roles and duties that we sometimes put our own well being on the back burner...and leave it there. There is so much pressure, (much of it self inflicted), to be perfect partners, friends, lovers, wives, mothers, employees or bosses, and we had better look good doing it too! Can we make dinner tonight? Of course! Can we drop the kids off at school and pick them up from baseball practice? You bet! Can we meet the girlfriends for coffee this evening? Wouldn't miss it! What about attending little Willies 3rd birthday party? I'll bring the piñata! Oh and can you work an extra hour tonight? Sure. Don't forget to hit the gym at some point either. And hey baby, can we make sweet, sweet love all night long after the dishes are done, the kids are asleep, you've taken a shower, and finished the wedding invitations you promised your sister you would help address? GAAAHHHH!

Sometimes, it's ok to say no. In fact, gracefully saying no is a well honed skill of Sensual Goddess. If you would rather stay home and take a long relaxing candlelit bubblebath that meet the girls at the bar after work, its ok to decline the invitation. If you don't want to take on the responsibility of organizing the soccer teams annual bake sale, don't. If you don't want to stay late at work again, politely but firmly explain that you already have made plans for the evening. You don't have to give more details than that. And never, *ever* have sex when you are not in the mood. This one can be tricky, especially for those in long term relationships, but it is important to honor yourself and your sexuality by not allowing your sensuality and your body to be used as a sexual vessel when you are really not feeling it, even if it is with the love of your life. Any sexual partner you have needs to understand that you have needs and desires as well, and sometimes, a solid nights sleep trumps a tumble in the sheets. Thats just the way it is, and there is no shame in that. And don't worry, as you get better at saying no and making room for yourself in your own life, as you learn to awaken and embrace the Sensual Woman within you, you will find you *do* want to make love all night long, more often than you'd think!

SOULWORK ASSIGNMENT:

Today, say NO to at least one thing you would normally say yes to out of duty or obligation, not desire. This can be a request from a friend, family member, or person at work, or it can be to yourself as well. For example, if you normally tell yourself "I'm going to call Grandma Jean because I always call her on Wednesday nights so she can tell me how bad her bunions are and remind me how infrequently I visit her." Tell yourself, "No. Not tonight. I am going to eat a bowl of strawberries in cream while watching "Chocolate" instead and I'm not going to feel one ounce of guilt doing it!" You go girl!

Day 20- Bathing in the Moonlight

Ahhh moonlight. The moon has long been linked to femininity and sensuality. It is a symbol of womanhood, the changing tides of our bodies and emotions, the cool mysteries of life, and the ebb and flow of life, death, and rebirth. The moon represents the Goddess in many traditions and belief systems. Moonlight is commonly used to cleanse and recharge crystals and gems, and aside from all this, few can deny the simple enchantment of a moonlit meadow, garden, or beach. Todays exercise is simple: Indulge in a relaxing moonlit bath.

SOULWORK ASSIGNMENT:

Take a moon bath! This is best done during the waxing moon, (the period of time in which the moon is in the process of growing larger), when the moon is at least half to completely full. There are a few different ways to do this, so go with the one that makes you the most comfortable. If you are doing this inside, try to find a room with a window that allows ample moonlight to stream through. Turn off all the lights and remove all your cloths. Lay on either a bed, couch, or pile of pillows and blankets where you can stretch out and allow the moonlight to wash over your body. If you have a large window in your bathroom and a nice tub, you can do this exercise in an actual bath, which is quite delightful. Feel free to add some rose petals or lavender sprigs to the water as well.

This exercise is even more profound if you are able to do it outside. If you are fortunate enough to have cooperative weather and a private yard, I strongly recommend taking advantage of it. If you have a swimming pool or access to a sheltered body of water, few things are as sensual as skinny dipping in moonlight laced waters. The purpose of this exercise is rest and relaxation. A chance to let go thoughts and stresses and indulge in the cleansing, healing properties of the moon while connecting with your feminine essence and allowing yourself to feel like a Goddess. If the moon is waxing or dark, or too small to give off much light, simply acknowledge its presence by observing it outside or through your window for a few moments, taking note of its position, curves, colors, and make a note to make time for your moon bath when she is full once more.

Day 21- Going Slow

Pay attention folks, todays lesson is *very* important. Are you ready? It's all about taking it slooooow. We live in such a fast paced society. Everything around us seems to be moving at light speed. We have an infinite amount of information available at our fingertips *instantly,* from pretty much anywhere on the planet. We start to get antsy if a web page takes longer than 10 seconds to load. Our food is fast. Service is fast. We drive fast. We talk fast. We are pushed to work fast. We wake up fast. We eat and drink fast. We even have sex fast, striving for orgasm almost as soon as we have engaged in the act. This is a big no no for Sensual Goddess. Sensual Goddess does not hurry. She takes her time. She takes things slowly. She stops to smell the roses.

She extends her moments of pleasure rather than rushing through them. As a result, she is able to experience a much wider array of sensual and pleasurable experiences throughout her day. She notices beautiful details. She authentically engages with those around her. She is an active participant in her life and privy to many wonderful scenarios that she would have otherwise missed had she been rushing. She fully inhabits the Now by savoring each and every moment.

SOULWORK ASSIGNMENT:

Slow down. Whatever it is you are doing, remind yourself to slow down several times throughout the day. Eat slowly. Chew your food completely. Drink with reverence. Walk at a leisurely pace. Feel how your body moves and allow your hips to sway. Slow your breath. Breathe deeply and fully. Instead of rushing through your shower and personal hygiene routine, extend it, luxuriate in it. Slowly lather and massage each and every part of your body. Dry yourself carefully and gently, and take your time rubbing lotion over every inch of your bare skin. Take your time cooking dinner. Enjoy the different smells and tastes you experience as you work, and when it comes to the bedroom…slow way down. Whether with a partner or self loving, let go of the desire to quickly climax, move slowly.

Give your body time to tell you what it is that it really wants. Find pleasure in the sensation of intimate touch, whether or not it is bringing you closer to the edge. Keep your breathing deep and steady. Keep your movements slow and sensual. Stay present, and afterwards, write about your experiences in your Goddess Diary.

It may initially feel like the world will stop turning if you stop moving at hyper speed. It won't. In fact, it will become a much more vivid, engaging, and beautiful place to live and love.

WEEK 4: BECOMING THE GODDESS

Now that you have awakened your inner Sensual Goddess, it is time to fully embody her; to become the Goddess you have always been and claim your birthright as a wildly divine and sexy being. Are you ready? You bet you are! Congratulations on making it this far, and enjoy integrating your Sensual Goddess fully into your life, so that she is you and you are her, and everything becomes dusted with the shimmering glow of your sensual, radiant feminine sexuality.

Day 22- Goddess Dancing

Dance is often described as a form of moving meditation. It has also been used as a form of ritual and release since time immemorial. Goddess dance is a beautiful and freeing way to let the mind fade into the background and allow the body to lead. As a full fledged Sensual Goddess, it is important to connect with, honor, and respect the physical body on a regular basis. This of course includes integrating some of the techniques you have already learned throughout this course, eating well, sleeping enough, and getting enough exercise. But it is equally important to celebrate the body simply for being. To allow it to move in ways it wants to without criticism or judgment. To accept that it is perfect right now, in this moment, just the way it is.

SOULWORK ASSIGNMENT:

I call this technique Goddess Dancing, to remind the participant that she (or he) is a manifestation of the divine and is entitled to celebrate themselves as such. Few activities are as fun or therapeutic as dance, which has been scientifically proven to have a plethora of health benefits ranging from mental/emotional to physical.

All you need to participate in Goddess Dancing for yourself is a big enough space, though tons of space is not necessary, (I have even danced while locked away in my tiny bathroom, listening to music on my iPhone when household/ family duties made it hard for me to catch my breath much less have a moment to myself), music that speaks to you, and anything else you want to include to set the mood, such as candles, incense, bellydance skirts or hip scarves, or elaborate face paint. Make it as intricate or as simple as you like. As always, feel free to do this in the buff if you feel so inclined. Now turn on your music and dance! Technique does not matter. No one is watching, (unless of course you want them to). This is your time and your space. Use your whole body if possible. Your head, neck, arms and hands. Of course pay attention to the way your hips and pelvis want to move, often in flowing, rolling, and undulating sensations that are extremely sexy and often cause for restraint and/or embarrassment when dancing in public. Let those inhibitions go. You are free to be as sexual in your movements as you like. Or, if you feel like dancing like a robot, do that! This exercise is all about listening to your body and letting it move in ways that feel good. Dance for as long as you like. When you are finished, write about your experience in your Goddess Diary.

Day 23- A Date with Self

This one may have made you uncomfortable in the past, but no longer! You are a Sensual Goddess and more than comfortable with treating yourself as such. You enjoy it. You are at home in your skin and at ease in your own company. And today, you are going to reinforce this new you by taking yourself on a date!

SOULWORK ASSIGNMENT:

Date yourself. Go out to eat alone and don't allow yourself to be uncomfortable or fidget with your cell phone! Be sure to order dessert. Or go solo to a movie you've been wanting to see, go shopping and buy yourself ice cream, or go and get that often talked about but rarely realized massage. Better yet, spend the day at a spa. You can also take yourself to the beach, go on a hike, or pack a picnic for one. The point is to get some quality YOU time and pampering in, delivered by none other than yourself. As a Sensual Goddess you do not wait for others to treat you like a queen. You are skilled and adapt at doing this all on your own, and find immense pleasure in it. You are also comfortable moving through the world and being seen on your own, without the need for a security blanket in the form of another person. You are strong, beautiful, and capable even, (and especially), by yourself. You do not need another's validation or justification to be radiant and cared for. After all, who knows what you like and want better than yourself? Especially after all the soul work you have done thus far!

Write about your date in your Diary, and just like everything else you are learning, don't forget to make this exercise a regular part of your self care routine.

Day 24- Spending Time in Nature

From our homes, to our cars, to our offices, we are so used to being apart from nature that it is easy to forget that we are *a part* of nature. No amount of glass and concrete can separate us from this fact. The natural world is Sensual

Goddess's domain, for she has come home to herself and realizes the intimate connection between all things, from her monthly cycles and the changing moon, her emotions to the movements of the heavens, and her body to the physical earth. She lets Mother Nature be her teacher and guide, and from her learns many important life lessons.

Spend some time in nature, and you will learn about balance. You will see that nature is not rushed, it moves slowly and at its own pace, regardless of the chaos surrounding it. You will notice nature is content just to be, with nothing to prove. A tree is content to be a tree, a daisy does not compare itself to a rose, a hawk does not try to become a sparrow. You will see that nature gracefully and fearlessly embraces the never ending cycle of birth, death, and rebirth, as seen in the seasons, the life of a butterfly, the growing and harvesting of a garden. Nature is sensual and full to the brim of sexuality, the essence of life and vitality. Nature knows no shame in sex and offers no apologies. It harnesses this creative power and burst forth with blossoming life time and time again, no matter how harsh the mountain winters or how fiery the desert summers.

SOULWORK ASSIGNMENT:

Get outside. Preferably for at least 90 minutes. The more the better, however 15 minutes is better than none at all. Spend some time simply being, observing, and enjoying. The wilder the landscape the better, but this can also be done in your backyard, the local park, a sidewalk cafe, or your apartment balcony in a pinch. Breathe in the fresh air, feel the sunlight or the chilly breeze, let it become a part of you. What natural sounds do you hear? Birds? The breeze? Water? What natural elements do you see? A weed pushing up through the sidewalk? A dragonfly zipping past or a spider crawling up a tree trunk? Do not attempt to judge or label. Be content with allowing yourself to become a part of all the natural world around you. Let yourself be calmed or energized by nature as you need. Thank her for all her beauty and all her healing. Feel pride at being a part of it.

Day 25- Desire Hunt

Desire is like fuel for Sensual Goddess. It is the spark that starts the fire, the enticing aroma that leads you to try an exciting new dish, the intoxicating music that beckons you to dance with the crowd of strangers in a courtyard plaza concert. Desire is what enables us to live fully through the senses, to BE a Sensual being. To embrace our Goddess potential. Today, we are going to pay homage to *your* unique desires, and maybe, if you feel up to it, give in to one or two. Or many ;)

SOULWORK ASSIGNMENT:

Think of todays activity as a sort of scavenger hunt, only much juicier! Today you will be looking for and taking note of everything that turns you on. Begin by writing in your Goddess Diary. You have full permission to list *everything* that makes your senses tingle. The color of the flowers blooming along the road. The shine and sparkle of your wedding ring. The soft touch of a warm blanket against your cheek. The sound of thunder signaling an approaching storm. The smell of a new book as you flip through the pages for the first time. The energetic zing that shoots through your body when you make eye contact with a cute stranger while running errands. Write down everything you can think of. Now ask yourself: What is it I desire right NOW? Write down your response. Take some time to think about whether or not you want to act on this desire or simply let its magic permeate your body and soul. For example, say the day is hot and sunny and what you really want to do is sunbathe naked. You can either acknowledge that desire, let it run through you, and say "Ahhh yes…that sounds absolutely wonderful. I hear you desire, I feel you. Thank you for being a part of my life." Or you can strip down and roll out the beach towel or lawn chair.

As you move on throughout the day, continue adding, either mentally or physically, to your list. Frequently ask yourself the question "What is it I desire NOW?" and make a conscious choice about what to do with this tantalizing energy. Reflect on all the many ways your senses are enlivened and emboldened. Be amazed at how open to and receptive to pleasure you have become.

Day 26- Creating a Sensual Goddess Vision Board

Vision boards are wonderful because they tap into our subconscious mind on a deep level via symbolism. They are a simple and powerful tool used to turn dreams and desires into reality. When you surround yourself with positive images of what it is you want, your reality changes to match those potent emotions of desire. This is because, based on the law of attraction, like attracts like when it comes to energetic vibrations, (I.E., a smile is likely to illicit a smile in response, and a frown will often be returned with a frown). By creating and displaying a personalized vision board in a place you will see it often, you are easily and frequently giving your subconscious, (and thus your *vibe*), a tune up, to ensure you are emitting those positive vibrations that will attract more of what you want into your life.

SOULWORK ASSIGNMENT:

Create your Sensual Goddess vision board. You will need poster or foam board, glue, scissors, and images and/ or words from magazines or your printer. Your vision board should display everything you love about your Sensual Goddess, and everything she embodies that you want to make a permanent part of your life. Cut out pictures of beautiful, confident women, positive affirmations, sensual nude photography, tasteful images of couples you admire, body loving belly dancers, lacy lingerie, bold direct stares, healthy, active bodies in motion, beautiful landscapes or scenes from nature, ripe juicy fruit and brilliantly colored flowers, whatever it is that speak to you. Hang your vision board over your bed, in your bathroom, or place it on your Sensual Goddess shrine. Just be sure it is somewhere where it will be admired by you often.

Day 27- Initiating Love

One of the things a Sensual Goddess loves the most is spreading love wherever she goes. She knows that the more she gives the more she will receive, but gives her love freely because that act in itself makes her feel wonderful. When it comes to giving love, she is not afraid and she does not hold back.

SOULWORK ASSIGNMENT:

Today, make an effort to initiate love. This could take on various forms, from taking the lead in seducing your lover, giving your friend a hug just because, sending your parents a card letting them know how much you appreciate them, or complimenting a stranger for no other reason than making them feel good. Do not act with expectations or the intention of receiving anything in return. Do it simply for the joy of making the world a more positive place. Do it because it feels good to you. Write about your experience in your Goddess Diary.

Day 28- Making Time for you, DAILY!

You are a Goddess, a Queen, and a Sensual Woman. You know your worth and do *not* put yourself on the back burner. Your days may be full and you may have many responsibilities, but you know that one of your greatest responsibilities is to yourself. Therefore, you make a habit out of taking time for yourself, to nourish your body mind and spirit, *every* day.

SOULWORK ASSIGNMENT:

Make time for you. Even if it is only for 30 minutes.
Claim it. Demand it. Know you deserve it. You may do
whatever you like during this time. In fact doing just what you
want to is exactly the point. Maybe you want to draw or
paint. Maybe read or watch a romantic movie. You can go for
a walk, meditate, Goddess Dance, self-love, dress up, bake
your favorite cupcakes, write in your diary, whatever it is you
feel like doing. Do not get caught up doing something
because you think you *should*. Don't go for a jog because
you know you need to exercise, go for a jog because that is
what your body is really wanting to do. It is therefore
important to take a few moments and a few deep breaths to
check in with yourself before cashing in on your daily "Me
Time" so that you are truly in touch with yourself and your
desires and can reap the greatest good from these important
moments. Of course, never feel guilty about taking this time
for yourself. This is *your* life. *Your* journey and experience.
Those around you can only benefit from you taking care of
yourself so that you can put your best self forward into the
world. Get in the habit of taking Me Time daily. Try to shoot
for 30 minutes to an hour. Longer if possible or necessary. At

first those around you may resist this new habit, but remain firm and adamant. Before long, they will be just as used to your restful/creative daily ritual as you are, and admire you for being so confident in your wants and needs.

WEEK 5: CARING FOR YOUR TEMPLE

Cheers to you, Sensual Goddess, you have made it to week five! By now you have fully embraced your inner Goddess and integrated this natural part of yourself into your conscious daily life. You know that she has been part of you all along, and that you and Sensual Goddess are one and the same. It has simply taken some attention, introspection, and loving practice to bring her back to the forefront of your being, where she belongs. She may have been hidden in the shadows for some time, but she can never be completely stamped out, tamed, or ignored. That is why you are reading this now. You knew in your heart it was time for her to fully emerge, and I congratulate you on your courage and commitment to self.

This last week is all about caring for your Goddess's temple, your very own body. This is where the Sensual Goddess resides, this is where she receives her pleasure and experiences the tantalizing physical sensations of the world around her. By treating your body as a holy object, a sacred space, you are giving yourself the honesty and respect that each of us deserves. You are taking responsibility for your health and well-being, and claiming your power as a woman of the earth.

Day 29- Walk

Walking is underrated. When it comes to health and fitness, so much emphasis is given to jogging, weightlifting, and burning calories, that we often forget the simple fact that the human body was designed to walk. Walking is a gentle and low-impact way to lose weight, increase metabolism, strengthen the immune system, tone muscles, build stronger bones and joints, relieve stress, boost cardio health, increase energy, and enhance self-esteem. In addition to this, exercising in nature increases oxygen intake, allows for more sensory stimulation, increases feelings of well-being and lowers depression. It triggers the primal regions of our brain and psyche, and raises serotonin levels.

SOULWORK ASSIGNMENT:

Go for a 15-30 minute walk. Longer if you are able to. If you can, do this without headphones, and observe the sounds of nature and the people around you. Aim to make this part of you daily routine, at least 4 to 5 days a week. You will soon begin to notice many of the above mentioned benefits.

Day 30- Stretching

Ahhh stretching, another wonderful form of fitness that, in my humble opinion, is not given enough credit. Flexible muscles prevent everyday injury by allowing a wider range of motion and movement for your joints, bones, and muscles. It improves posture and allows you to feel more calm, open, free, and confident. You are able to travel and move about more comfortably and can sit and position your body with ease in many different positions that would otherwise be challenging and uncomfortable. Can you see why this would be an important aspect of fitness for Sensual Goddess, (wink-wink)? Her limber body allows her to move with feline grace and confidence and keeps her Prana, or energetic life force, moving freely and uninhibited. In this way, she can use her body to express a much wider range of emotions and desires, and welcome many more pleasurable sensations into her reality as well.

SOULWORK ASSIGNMENT:

Stretch. I recommend stretching for at least 30 minutes a day. Many people find it easier to stretch muscles that have already been warmed up, so you may want to try jogging in place, doing some jumping jacks, or dancing to one or two of your favorite songs before you begin. The import thing is to listen to your body, which by now, you are much more comfortable doing. Take time to stretch your legs, hips, back, shoulders, neck, and arms. Consider taking a yoga class or looking up a beginners stretching routine online. Your body, and spirit, will thank you.

Day 31- Diet

This one is hard for many people. It can be difficult to break away from habits of eating that have been in place for years, if not an entire lifetime. It is important to remember that you really are what you eat. If you are eating dead, chemical laced food, you will feel dead/low on energy, and often cranky or irritable. If you are eating *real*, ethically obtained, chemical free and from-the-earth food, you will feel energetic, vibrant, healthy, and strong. Remember that your body is a temple. Do NOT forget this! It deserves only the highest quality, healthiest, most nourishing of daily offerings. Make every attempt to limit sugar and stay away from processed foods. Health is wealth, not just to the Sensual Goddess, but to everyone. However, many of us often take it for granted until we are feeling ill or develop disease. Even more than exercise, a healthy diet, which includes plenty of fresh water, is the foundation of a healthy body *and* mind. Food is truly magical in that it has the ability to transform us from the inside out, and isn't it wonderful that *we* are in control of what we choose to take into our bodies. Much like with the lovers we choose to embrace, much care and consideration should be given to the items we eat and drink. This aspect of self care should never be overlooked.

SOULWORK ASSIGNEMENT:

For the next 24 hours track your diet in your Goddess Diary. When you are done, take some time to go over what you have eaten and whether or not this is typical of your day to day diet. Where do you do well and where is there room for improvement. Be honest with yourself. Consider researching some well known health promoting diets such as a whole foods diets, paleo, or gluten and dairy free. As always, listen to your body and consult a health care professional if you are wanting to make any drastic changes to your eating routine, especially if you are nursing, pregnant, or taking medications.

Day 32- Vaginal Massage

This may sound a little intimidating at first, but never fear. With a little practice you will be an expert in no time.

As women, much of our stress and tension is carried in our pelvis, our Yoni (the sanskrit word for vagina, meaning "sacred space", which I love!), and our reproductive organs. To make matters worse, this stress comes not only from our own experiences, but can also be inherited from past traumas and abuses endured by our ancestors as well as the female collective consciousness! Yet there is no need to panic. With time and attention even the wounds of our lineage and global atrocities can be alleviated.

Much like tension carried in the neck and shoulders, unresolved tension that we carry in our feminine core can lead to muscle stiffness and imbalance. Many women who suffer from limited sensation, numbness, or pain during intercourse have no idea that most, if not all of these symptoms can be easily removed with the simple self care practice of vaginal massage. Vaginal massage not only relieves muscle tension in the same way a shoulder or back massage does, but it increases blood flow, sensitivity, and vitality to our most sacred place and connects us intimately to the root of our womanhood.

<u>SOULWORK ASSIGNMENT:</u>

Give yourself a vaginal massage! The goal here is not sexual stimulation, although if that happens, great! Go with it if it feels right!

Find a place and time where you will not be disturbed for at least an hour and get into a comfortable position. Carefully insert your index finger into your yoni and moving from the front, (behind your pubic bone and underneath your urethra), to the back (behind your tailbone and perineum), in a clockwise position, begin to gently apply pressure to the walls of your vagina while paying attention to any sensation, or lack thereof, that you experience. Begin with the area just inside your vagina opening, taking extra care to not apply too much pressure to 12 O'clock and 6 O'clock, as the tissues in these areas are thinner and more easily irritated. Gradually move deeper as you feel comfortable. If you encounter any tender areas or places of pain, take slow, deep breaths and carefully use your finger to massage the area the way you would a painful shoulder until the discomfort diminishes or ceases altogether. Give the same treatment to areas of muted sensation or numbness. Lack of sensation often results from past sexual abuses or traumas, where as a result, the mind disassociates from the body. Thus it is important to be aware of any emotions or repressed feelings you experience while preforming this exercise. It is important to let them come to the surface so that they may be released. If you feel like crying, cry. If you want to laugh, laugh. Be gentle with and loving with yourself and remind yourself that you are a physical manifestation of a Goddess, and that it is time to release old tensions and hurts that are no longer serving you and may be blocking your capacity for pleasure and joy.

Try to give yourself a vaginal massage at least once a week. You will notice an increased sense of health and power stemming from your core, a greater sense of connection to your personal sexuality, and an overall increased sense of well-being.

Write about your experiences in your Goddess Diary to be able to easily recognize patterns and reference your progress.

Day 33- Breast Massage

In Tantra, the breasts are the positive pole of the female body, the yoni being the negative. In other words, the breast/heart are where we project forth our love and energy, and the Yoni is where we receive love and energy. The opposite is true for males, whose positive pole is the penis, or lingam, and whose negative or receptive pole is the chest/ heart. When the two meet in harmonious sexual union, there is a naturally powerful and healing circular flow of energy between the two bodies. In Tantra, it is believed that the breasts must be properly caressed and stimulated before the yoni can become ready to receive the lingam, otherwise the sexual energy will not circulate properly and the whole experience will fall flat, (or at least not be as enjoyable or beneficial as possible). With proper attention and stimulation, the breast can experience extreme sensations of pleasure and it is even possible for many women to have an orgasm from breast stimulation alone!

In addition, the breasts are also a symbol of womanhood and motherhood, (bear in mind that motherhood is *not* exclusive from Sensual Goddess or a womans' sexuality). We are nourished, fed, and comforted from our mothers breasts, and give our own children this same miraculous gift. Our breasts are the physical representation of our robust and ample capacity to nourish and sustain life, to love, and to give freely of ourselves. Their size, shape and appearance is as diverse and beautiful as the woman they belong to.

Because of our media driven culture, many women feel insecure or critical towards this beautiful part of their body. It it time to stop this mentality. It is time to take back our power and love and admire this empowering part of our female body. It is time to stop judging, comparing, and criticizing, and to pay some special attention to our "girls" and give them a little well deserved TLC.

SOULWORK ASSIGNMENT:

Give yourself a breast massage! I find it best to do this sans bra, and it feels absolutely wonderful if you have just removed your bra after a long day. You can stand topless in front of a mirror or simply sit or lay back in a comfortable position. Close your eyes if you like. Then, simply place your hands on your breasts and begin to rub, caress, and massage them in any way that feels good to you. Experiment with different strokes and pressures. Let your breasts tell you what feels wonderful and what does not. Send them tender, loving, appreciative thoughts as you do this. Talk to them! Develop a relationship with them! Let them know they are beautiful and perfect just as they are. Get them used to being touched and appreciated in a loving and compassionate manner. You can do this every day if you like, and the benefits include increase blood flow to your breasts, (which could increase their size and firmness, if thats something you care about), becoming familiar with their shape and texture, so that any irregularities will be easily noticed, and increasing sensitivity and capacity for pleasure, which of course, can be delightful when it comes to lovemaking. The better you know your breasts, and what it is they like, the easier it is for you to translate their wants and desires to your lover. It's a win-win for all parties involved!

Day 34- Self Massage

We've done the Yoni. we've done the breasts. But what about the rest of our body? Of course, while the breast and vagina may be akin to glorious and sacred shines within, our entire body is a temple, as we have already come to realize. And it deserves as many loving touches and caresses as our very special lady parts. Self massage is fun and easy. It is a simple way of showing gratitude to our physical body, of letting it know we love and appreciate all it does for us. By regularly practicing self-massage, we are sending a powerful subconscious message to ourselves and our inner Goddess. One that says we are worthy, deserving, and accepting of pleasure, health, pampering, and unconditional love.

SOULWORK ASSIGNMENT:

Self massage can pretty much be done anywhere and can be as simple or as decadent as you like. It can be done at work by simply taking a moment to breathe deep and rub out a tense spot in your neck, on the subway by using one hand to fully massage the palm and each finger of the other, in the shower by taking some extra time to really massage your scalp as you rinse out your shampoo, or on the couch where you knead the soles of your feet as you watch TV.

Of course, I am an advocate of reeaaallly pampering yourself to the fullest, without distractions, and so I recommend as often as possible, giving yourself a full fledged, total body massage while laying naked on silk sheets, using lotions, oils, calming music, and flickering candles. Start at your feet. Don't rush. Sensual Goddess never rushes. Take your time and work your way up each leg, to your hips, your butt, your torso, arms, neck, and finishing with your face and head. I assure you, you will feel simply divine when you are finished.

Day 35- Honoring YOU

Congratulations Sensual Goddess, you've done it! Today is the last day of your 5 week long course. Take a moment to let it sink in, and reflect on how far you have come. Feel proud at having given yourself this gift of empowerment and committing to living a life that overflows with pleasure and sensuality. Know that there will always be something more to learn, and your capacity for joy, love, and pleasure is truly infinite. Take time daily to check in with your heart and with your body. Use your confidence and womanhood to inspire those around you. Give love freely and fearlessly. You are already making the world a better place, simply by being you, and I applaud you, sister, friend, and fellow Goddess.

SOULWORK ASSIGNMENT:

Do something today that honors you and this path you have chosen. Today is a celebration of YOU! Treat yourself appropriately. Buy yourself a beautiful bouquet of flowers or pretty piece of jewelry you've been admiring. Take the day off of work and go to the beach or on a nice hike. Add your own picture to your Sensual Goddess shrine or go and get your hair done or a sexy new cut. Write yourself a love letter or heartfelt piece of poetry honoring your Sensual Goddess. Do a random act of kindness and remain anonymous if possible. Write in your diary, invite your girlfriends over for a dance party, or buy some new lingerie. Do whatever it is that makes you feel WONDERFUL! Because you are wonderful, divine, and oh so SENSUAL!

ABOUT THE AUTHOR

S.R. Lee is a Mother, Lover, Tantra & Sensuality Coach, Reiki Master, Ordained Spiritual Counselor & a fantasy loving Wild Witch who practices in the High Deserts of Southern California. She is working on developing her permaculture village & tribe, and dreams of riding a wild mustang. You can find her at:

www.thewitchwriter.com

Note From the Author:

Dear Sensual Goddess,
If you enjoyed this book please take a moment to post a honest review on amazon.com. This gesture would be appreciated beyond words.

For additional content, free updates, personal correspondence, and an inside look at my latest projects, I would like to invite you to become a part of the tribe by subscribing to my private email list at www.thewitchwriter.com

I cannot wait to hear from you, and look forward to getting to know YOU, where your passions lie, and what hopes and dreams you nurture whilst on your sensually wild path. Goddess Bless.

Yours in Deepest Gratitude,

S. R. Lee

Please enjoy this free sample of S.R. Lees'
revolutionary upcoming book, "How to F-ck Like a
Goddess", available February, 2019. Be sure to
subscribe at www.thewitchwriter.com for upcoming
events and release dates.

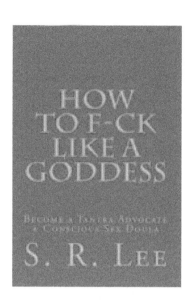

How to F-ck
Like a Goddess
Become a Tantra Advocate &
Conscious Sex Doula

By: S. R. Lee

Table Of Contents

PART 1: TEACHING TANTRA AND SETTING UP YOUR OWN BUSINESS

Congratulations! If you are reading this it means that you have decided to pursue the path of becoming a conscious sex instructor, coach, teacher, or my favorite term, *doula.* Traditionally a doula is a woman who is trained to provide another woman with any informational, emotional, and physical support she and her family may need through the life-changing rite of passage that is giving birth. To me, because of the history and modern trends of woman's rights and birthing in our westernized country, this is an empowering term, and I would like to apply it here to the art of sex. For sex is truly where *all* life begins, and doulas are valued highly for the postpartum *and* pre-birth care of the mother and child. Why not start at the very beginning? Additionally, to witness a woman or a man truly coming into their own power as they finally accept, understand, and embrace their own unique sexuality, is much like watching a birth. There is anticipation, excitement, pain, struggle, sometimes fear (and it aint always pretty!). But there also support, trust, intuition, love, faith, and so much bliss. Being a matured human who is finally able to develop true skill in the divine art of sex, to be able to both give and receive simultaneously, unrestrained pleasure, can be an experience much like being reborn. There are few careers as rewarding or as *needed* in todays modern world as the Sex Doula.

In addition to the intrinsic satisfaction of helping people connect with their sexuality and reawaken their inherent joy at the decadence and juiciness of life and love, you will learn how to achieve financial freedom by working for yourself from the comfort of your own home, or anywhere else in the world for that matter. This offers up an huge amount of personal freedom, and you become not only financially independent, but able to make your own schedule, define your own coaching style, and choose exactly when and where you work.

The information presented in this manual is designed to give you the key informational elements you will need in order to begin assisting clients immediately.

While Tantra is a many faceted and ancient art form that can take many lifetimes to explore, the knowledge contained within these pages has been proven time and time again to have enormous positive effects on the quality of life for individuals and couples. Within the context of this book, the word *Tantra* will be used to refer to conscious sexual intercourse, (i.e. all parties involved are able to stay present in the moment and suspend interference from the mind).

Once you have read and understood the principals presented here, you may begin practicing them in earnest, making sure to document the process in a journal or video diary, for your own future benefit and those of the clients you will share this wisdom with. You alone can decide if you are truly ready to begin taking on paying students.

The first part of this manual will teach you the basics of becoming and being a Conscious Sex Doula . It will tell you how to make $400 or more per day, how to attract quality clients, and how to conduct a session.

In the second part of the manual you will learn the fundamentals of the art of Tantra itself, interpreted and described as I have come to understand and practice it through my personal studies, experiments, and experience. It is important that you have a firm and confident understanding of these principles yourself, especially if you hope to successfully coach others, so I *highly* recommend taking some time to explore and practice these ideas for yourself, as well as perhaps reading "Your Sensual Awakening" *before* you begin marketing yourself. There is absolutely no benefit to rushing the process. (In fact, to due so would run counter to everything that Tantra stands for). This is the best way to ensure your success as a highly trusted and sought after coach.

Let's get started!

WHAT IS TANTRA?

Simply put, Tantra is the merging of sex and meditation. It is an ancient practice thought to have originated in India. It is about raising and sustaining energy to empower love of self and connection with the Universe. Through Tantra, we are able to realize our own inherent perfection and that of our lovers as well.

In addition, Tantra has been shown to have numerous benefits outside of sexual bliss, including:

* healing past emotional wounds,
* alleviating anxiety and depression,
* empowering women by treating them with honor and respect,
* empowering men by teaching them to be more open, caring, and confident,
* enabling couples to achieve true satisfaction from sex and intimacy,
* transforming sex into a truly sacred and bliss filled experience,
* rejuvenating health and vitality,
* deepening our connection to others,
* making life more sensual, juicy, and beautiful, and...
* opening up our infinite capacity to express love and joy.

WHAT IS A SEX DOULA AND WHAT DO THEY DO?

A Conscious Sex Doula is someone who is intimately familiar with the theories and practices of Tantra, and who is able to easily articulate this knowledge in a way that is accessible to their clients and students, many of which may be seeking solutions to issues such as sexual disconnect, disinterest, impotence, or other such frustrations.

A Sex Doula may also work with clients who are perfectly content in their sexuality and sex lives, but may simply be curious to learn more about Tantra, grow their knowledge about this intimate art form, or expand on their own sensuality or spirituality.

Therefore, a Sex Doula not only teaches the art of Tantra itself, but aids her/his clients in awakening and connecting with themselves and others on deeper, more satisfactory levels. A Sex Doula shows them how to accept pleasure and recognize their own perfection, and guides and supports them along their unique journeys of self-discovery.

Made in the USA
Las Vegas, NV
10 January 2022

41035437R00059